# 1,000 Words to Get Started

FLASH FICTION LIVE PRESENTS
101 CREATIVE WRITING
PROMPTS & CHALLENGES

# 1,000 Words to Get Started

## FLASH FICTION LIVE PRESENTS 101 CREATIVE WRITING PROMPTS & CHALLENGES

**CHANDRA ARTHUR & NATALIE LOCKE**

INIMITABLE
BOOKS
UNFORGETTABLE STORIES

Published by Inimitable Books, LLC
www.inimitablebooksllc.com

1,000 WORDS TO GET STARTED.
Copyright © 2024 by Chandra Arthur & Natalie Locke.
All rights reserved. Printed in China.

Library of Congress Cataloguing-in-Publication Data is available.

First edition, 2024
Cover design by Mandi Lynn of River Bend Books

ISBN 978-1-958607-21-3 (paperback)
10 9 8 7 6 7 6 5 4 3 2 1

To that one random guy, who piped up amidst all the blaring horns and gave me some advice I will never forget, "Lady, you can't turn here."

~

Dedicated to my husband and children for enduring my chaos despite not always understanding it.

And to my sister in writing, Chandra Arthur.

# 1,000 Words to Get Started

Flex that artistic license when the prompt or challenges could go multiple directions. You can fill in the prompts' blanks with as many words as you want. Write in the book or outside to reuse the prompts in the future.

These stories are for you. The point is to try new things, knowing it will be rough. This is the time to test your writing skills instead of committing to a short story, novella, or novel. Don't worry about political correctness or not getting it "perfect." Just try.

You can write in your own words or pick any of the 1,000 words in the back of this book. If you're unsure where to start, pick the 10 words first (and put them in the provided box under each prompt), then select the prompt. Make it as random or as pre-planned as you're comfortable with.

There is only 1 rule: all writing must be under 1,000 words.

To make it more fun, you can also combine any of the prompts with one of the writing/environment challenges (write the number in the box next to any prompt).

Share your stories with us on social media with the hashtag: #1000wordsprompt.

*Tip to make prompts conflict based:*
• Negate a verb: e.g. "can" becomes "cannot" / "can't"
"Can't find the keys" carries differently than "Won't find the keys" or "Shouldn't find the keys"

*Tips to make prompts character based:*
- Abilities (lack of or super hero?)
- Recurring flashes or total memory loss?
- Profession (first day, day in the life, or want to leave?)
- Relationships (current, past, or hopeful future?)
- Goals (towards, achieved, fail but gain something else?)
- Age/maturity level (will it change at the end?)
- Blend into a crowd or stand out? (looks wise)
- What distinguishable personality traits do they have? (Opinionated, extrovert, quiet, workaholic, different project each week, etc)
- Faith? Vices?

For example: Compulsive gambler donates winnings to the poor, but doesn't have money to keep donating. The donations are the only thing keeping a shelter open. The gambler cares because their estranged mother was homeless when they were younger before she passed.

# 1,000 Words to Get Started

The prompts are filled in, but you can skip around in completing them as you see fit. If you're also doing a challenge, don't forget to write it into the little box in the top left corner of a prompt page.

## Writing Challenges:

1. Start each new sentence with the last word of the preceding sentence
2. Write a story with an unreliable narrator
3. Start & end the story with the same word (one of the 10)
4. Make the first word of each sentence in the flash create a "secret," coherent sentence on its own
5. Don't use any words with double letters (like stacked vowels or consonant, such as in letter)
6. Set the whole story in one room (no one enters or leaves) and real-time
7. Write in the horror or thriller genre
8. Write a children's story
9. Write in the romance genre
10. Write in the sci-fi genre
11. Write in the fantasy genre
12. Write a slice of life story
13. Write part of a memoir
14. Write a contemporary story
15. Pick a poem style to follow (haiku, rhyming, etc.)
16. Put as many of your 10 words in a single sentence
17. Write a story where time is moving backwards

18. Don't use "the" or "and" in your story
19. Write a story where all the characters are animals
20. Write a story only using dialogue (dialogue tags okay)
21. Write a story only using narrative (no dialogue)
22. Write a story twice (1,000 words total max) from 2 different perspectives
23. Use 1 of your selected words *10 times*; the other 9 words are each used once
24. The first and last line of the story have to be the *same*
25. Use synonyms of the 10 words instead of the words
26. Use antonyms of the 10 words instead of the words
27. Story set in a historical event (research may be required)
28. Remove all of your characters' sense of sight in the story
29. Remove all of your characters' hearing in the story
30. Use a previous flash fiction's side character and make them the main character in the same or different storyline
31. The main character is completely alone in your story
32. Chose a point of view completely different from your own gender, sexuality, religion, etc. (research may be required to avoid stereotypes)
33. Write from another character's perspective from an already written flash in this book
34. Have only unnamed characters in your story
35. Rewrite a flash with a new prompt and words
36. Write the story like a newscast (for radio or television)
37. Write an epistolary story (as letters between 2 parties—individual people or groups)

# 1,000 Words to Get Started

38. Write a story in second person ("You," not "I" or "S/he")
39. Write a story in first person (use "I")
40. Write a story in third person limited point of view
41. Write a story in third person omniscient point of view
42. Have the characters eat in the story (color, taste, texture)
43. Give the main character two options, explore them choosing each (1,000 words total max)
44. Have your story's timeline cover one minute
45. Have your story's timeline cover a week
46. Write a story where your main character is the villain
47. End your flash with a cliffhanger
48. Start your flash in the middle of an action sequence
49. Use as many clichés as possible in your story
50. Describe items in your story without using colors
51. Have your characters only communicate non-verbally
52. Use real famous people as your characters, sticking to their public personalities
53. Have your characters on an assembly line but don't repeat the description of the repetitive action
54. Have the main character search for 3 of the 10 words but not find them until then end
55. Scramble each of the 10 words, then make up a new context to use them in the world you created
56. Have everyone notice something about your character but they don't realize until the end
57. Write a story where everyone dies at the end
58. Have the protagonist lose something/someone important

59. Research a place you've only seen in photos/TV/Movies and set your story there

60. Have the first and last lines mean the *opposite*

61. Have your characters try to maintain a conversation while doing something complicated with their hands

62. Write 2 characters meeting each other for the first time

63. Write a story twice where the main character is the hero then in the same scene as the villain (max 1,000 words)

64. Write the story like a diary entry

65. Rewrite Challenge 64 (above) as prose in 3rd person omniscient point-of-view

66. The hero and villain meet each other without realizing it

67. Have a side character mimic the main character

68. Write from the perspective of an object a character uses

69. Have the main character working on a task but keep starting over because of repeated interruptions

70. Have the main character dream and notice something that alerts them it is a dream

71. Start your story with a question and unfold wrong answers until the very end where the right one is revealed

72. Jump between two scenes as they happen simultaneously

73. Write without using the vowel *e* (check your 10 words)

74. Write without using the vowel *i* (check your 10 words)

75. Write without using the vowel *o* (check your 10 words)

76. Write without using the vowel *a* (check your 10 words)

77. Write without using the vowel *u* (check your 10 words)

78. Write without using the vowel *y* (check your 10 words)

# 1,000 Words to Get Started

79. Write the story like a description on the back of a book
80. Write a story about a _____, using all synonyms for the word but never say the word
81. Create a story that can be read forward and backward
82. Write a story about high school (grades 9-12) but never say it is set at/about high school
83. Write a story where a source of light keeps moving (flashlight, car headlights, torch, etc.) and the focus of the scene changes/new details are revealed each time the light illuminates the space
84. Write a story where the main character communicates with someone who in a different location/time as them
85. The main character realizes they're the *side* character in someone else's story
86. Convey the characters are speaking in another language without writing in that language (try to avoid accent stereotypes in descriptions)
87. Have the main character create and implement a plan only to not succeed as expected
88. Have your story be a continuous loop where the end also can be the beginning

## Writing Environment Challenges:
89. Write at your normal time
90. Write right before breakfast
91. Write right before bed
92. Write right before or after lunch

93. Write in the middle of your normal sleep cycle
94. Write in complete silence
95. Write in a noisy space
96. Outline before you draft
97. Handwrite your story then type it (editing is acceptable in the transfer between mediums)
98. Pick a prompt and your 10 words, then write the story on a 30 minute timer
99. Type your story with your screen covered, then write it in this book (editing is acceptable in the transfer from screen to page)
100. Write a 500 word (minimum) story. Every time you cross into the next hundred, walk away from the story for at least an hour before you resume
101. Draft without an outline

# 1,000 Words to Get Started

Pick a place, a verb, a tree, an animal, a drink, a food, a number, a form of travel, a piece of furniture, and a profession and create your own prompt

# 1,000 Words to Get Started

_____

_____

_____

_____

_____

_____

_____

_____

_____

_____

_____

_____

_____

_____

_____

_____

_____

_____

_____

_____

_____

_____

_____

_____

_____

_____

_____

_____

_____

# 1,000 Words to Get Started

Start or end the story with the question "can you keep _____?"

_____
_____
_____

_____
_____
_____
_____
_____
_____
_____
_____
_____
_____
_____
_____
_____
_____
_____
_____
_____
_____

# 1,000 Words to Get Started

_____
_____
_____
_____
_____
_____
_____
_____
_____
_____
_____
_____
_____
_____
_____
_____
_____
_____
_____
_____
_____
_____
_____
_____
_____
_____
_____
_____
_____
_____
_____

# 1,000 Words to Get Started

Game of _____

# 1,000 Words to Get Started

_____

_____

_____

_____

_____

_____

_____

_____

_____

_____

_____

_____

_____

_____

_____

_____

_____

_____

_____

_____

_____

_____

_____

_____

_____

_____

_____

_____

# 1,000 Words to Get Started

The _____
changes plans

# 1,000 Words to Get Started

_____

_____

_____

_____

_____

_____

_____

_____

_____

_____

_____

_____

_____

_____

_____

_____

_____

_____

_____

_____

_____

_____

_____

_____

_____

_____

_____

_____

_____

_____

# 1,000 Words to Get Started

This isn't how _____
remember(s) it

# 1,000 Words to Get Started

_____

_____

_____

_____

_____

_____

_____

_____

_____

_____

_____

_____

_____

_____

_____

_____

_____

_____

_____

_____

_____

_____

_____

_____

_____

_____

_____

# 1,000 Words to Get Started

The _____ is on
the other _____

# 1,000 Words to Get Started

# 1,000 Words to Get Started

☐ _____ Earth forever

# 1,000 Words to Get Started

# 1,000 Words to Get Started

□ _____ revealed
before _____

_____

.................................................

.................................................

_____

_____

_____

_____

_____

_____

_____

_____

_____

_____

_____

_____

_____

_____

_____

_____

_____

_____

_____

_____

# 1,000 Words to Get Started

_____

_____

_____

_____

_____

_____

_____

_____

_____

_____

_____

_____

_____

_____

_____

_____

_____

_____

_____

_____

_____

_____

_____

_____

_____

_____

_____

_____

_____

_____

_____

_____

_____

# 1,000 Words to Get Started

☐ Unexplained _____

# 1,000 Words to Get Started

# 1,000 Words to Get Started

What _____
in the _____

# 1,000 Words to Get Started

# 1,000 Words to Get Started

☐ Trying _____

# 1,000 Words to Get Started

_____

_____

_____

_____

_____

_____

_____

_____

_____

_____

_____

_____

_____

_____

_____

_____

_____

_____

_____

_____

_____

_____

_____

_____

_____

_____

_____

_____

# 1,000 Words to Get Started

☐ Our last _____

# 1,000 Words to Get Started

_____

_____

_____

_____

_____

_____

_____

_____

_____

_____

_____

_____

_____

_____

_____

_____

_____

_____

_____

_____

_____

_____

_____

_____

_____

_____

# 1,000 Words to Get Started

The _____

before the picture was taken

# 1,000 Words to Get Started

# 1,000 Words to Get Started

What the _____

was really for _____

# 1,000 Words to Get Started

_____

_____

_____

_____

_____

_____

_____

_____

_____

_____

_____

_____

_____

_____

_____

_____

_____

_____

_____

_____

_____

_____

_____

_____

_____

_____

_____

_____

_____

_____

_____

# 1,000 Words to Get Started

_____ was framed

# 1,000 Words to Get Started

_____

_____

_____

_____

_____

_____

_____

_____

_____

_____

_____

_____

_____

_____

_____

_____

_____

_____

_____

_____

_____

_____

_____

_____

_____

_____

_____

_____

_____

_____

# 1,000 Words to Get Started

☐ _____ while waiting

# 1,000 Words to Get Started

# 1,000 Words to Get Started

_____ surgery

# 1,000 Words to Get Started

---
---
---
---
---
---
---
---
---
---
---
---
---
---
---
---
---
---
---
---
---
---
---
---
---
---
---
---
---
---

# 1,000 Words to Get Started

Reality or _____

# 1,000 Words to Get Started

_____

_____

_____

_____

_____

_____

_____

_____

_____

_____

_____

_____

_____

_____

_____

_____

_____

_____

_____

_____

_____

_____

_____

_____

_____

_____

_____

# 1,000 Words to Get Started

☐ _____ under the

_____

_____
_____

# 1,000 Words to Get Started

_____
_____
_____
_____
_____
_____
_____
_____
_____
_____
_____
_____
_____
_____
_____
_____
_____
_____
_____
_____
_____
_____
_____
_____
_____
_____
_____
_____

# 1,000 Words to Get Started

Got to be _____

# 1,000 Words to Get Started

_____

_____

_____

_____

_____

_____

_____

_____

_____

_____

_____

_____

_____

_____

_____

_____

_____

_____

_____

_____

_____

_____

_____

_____

_____

_____

_____

_____

_____

_____

_____

# 1,000 Words to Get Started

Incoming _____

# 1,000 Words to Get Started

# 1,000 Words to Get Started

Thought _____
was/were alone

# 1,000 Words to Get Started

_____
_____
_____
_____
_____
_____
_____
_____
_____
_____
_____
_____
_____
_____
_____
_____
_____
_____
_____
_____
_____
_____
_____
_____
_____
_____
_____
_____
_____
_____
_____
_____
_____
_____

# 1,000 Words to Get Started

popped

# 1,000 Words to Get Started

# 1,000 Words to Get Started

☐ _____ and lost

# 1,000 Words to Get Started

_____

_____

_____

_____

_____

_____

_____

_____

_____

_____

_____

_____

_____

_____

_____

_____

_____

_____

_____

_____

_____

_____

_____

_____

_____

_____

_____

_____

# 1,000 Words to Get Started

☐ Thrill _____
seeks

# 1,000 Words to Get Started

_____

_____

_____

_____

_____

_____

_____

_____

_____

_____

_____

_____

_____

_____

_____

_____

_____

_____

_____

_____

_____

_____

_____

_____

_____

_____

# 1,000 Words to Get Started

_____ the
_____ star

# 1,000 Words to Get Started

# 1,000 Words to Get Started

☐ _____ the way

# 1,000 Words to Get Started

_____

_____

_____

_____

_____

_____

_____

_____

_____

_____

_____

_____

_____

_____

_____

_____

_____

_____

_____

_____

_____

_____

_____

_____

_____

_____

_____

_____

_____

# 1,000 Words to Get Started

☐ What's _____

# 1,000 Words to Get Started

# 1,000 Words to Get Started

_____ places

# 1,000 Words to Get Started

_____

_____

_____

_____

_____

_____

_____

_____

_____

_____

_____

_____

_____

_____

_____

_____

_____

_____

_____

_____

_____

_____

_____

_____

_____

_____

_____

_____

_____

# 1,000 Words to Get Started

☐ _____ point

# 1,000 Words to Get Started

_____

_____

_____

_____

_____

_____

_____

_____

_____

_____

_____

_____

_____

_____

_____

_____

_____

_____

_____

_____

_____

_____

_____

_____

_____

_____

_____

_____

_____

_____

_____

# 1,000 Words to Get Started

When walls _____

# 1,000 Words to Get Started

_____
_____
_____
_____
_____
_____
_____
_____
_____
_____
_____
_____
_____
_____
_____
_____
_____
_____
_____
_____
_____
_____
_____
_____
_____
_____
_____
_____

# 1,000 Words to Get Started

What the _____
hides

# 1,000 Words to Get Started

_____

_____

_____

_____

_____

_____

_____

_____

_____

_____

_____

_____

_____

_____

_____

_____

_____

_____

_____

_____

_____

_____

_____

_____

_____

_____

_____

_____

_____

_____

# 1,000 Words to Get Started

The clock is _____

# 1,000 Words to Get Started

# 1,000 Words to Get Started

☐ Hands _____

# 1,000 Words to Get Started

_____

_____

_____

_____

_____

_____

_____

_____

_____

_____

_____

_____

_____

_____

_____

_____

_____

_____

_____

_____

_____

_____

_____

_____

_____

_____

_____

_____

_____

_____

# 1,000 Words to Get Started

☐ _____ with a story

┌─────────────────────────────────────────────┐
│ ............................................. │
│ ............................................. │
└─────────────────────────────────────────────┘

_____

_____

_____

_____

_____

_____

_____

_____

_____

_____

_____

_____

_____

_____

_____

_____

_____

_____

# 1,000 Words to Get Started

_____
_____
_____
_____
_____
_____
_____
_____
_____
_____
_____
_____
_____
_____
_____
_____
_____
_____
_____
_____
_____
_____
_____
_____
_____
_____
_____
_____
_____
_____

# 1,000 Words to Get Started

Before _____

or _____

# 1,000 Words to Get Started

# 1,000 Words to Get Started

☐ A childhood _____ 's story

# 1,000 Words to Get Started

# 1,000 Words to Get Started

☐ ———————————————————— too many

# 1,000 Words to Get Started

# 1,000 Words to Get Started

□ _____ later

# 1,000 Words to Get Started

_____
_____
_____
_____
_____
_____
_____
_____
_____
_____
_____
_____
_____
_____
_____
_____
_____
_____
_____
_____
_____
_____
_____
_____
_____
_____
_____
_____

# 1,000 Words to Get Started

Your word is _____

# 1,000 Words to Get Started

_____
_____
_____
_____
_____
_____
_____
_____
_____
_____
_____
_____
_____
_____
_____
_____
_____
_____
_____
_____
_____
_____
_____
_____
_____
_____
_____
_____
_____

# 1,000 Words to Get Started

☐ _____wasn't planned

# 1,000 Words to Get Started

# 1,000 Words to Get Started

_____ help

# 1,000 Words to Get Started

# 1,000 Words to Get Started

When _____ matter

# 1,000 Words to Get Started

_____
_____
_____
_____
_____
_____
_____
_____
_____
_____
_____
_____
_____
_____
_____
_____
_____
_____
_____
_____
_____
_____
_____
_____
_____
_____
_____
_____
_____
_____
_____

# 1,000 Words to Get Started

_____ condition

# 1,000 Words to Get Started

# 1,000 Words to Get Started

The _____ reunion

# 1,000 Words to Get Started

# 1,000 Words to Get Started

Family's _____

# 1,000 Words to Get Started

# 1,000 Words to Get Started

Upside _____

# 1,000 Words to Get Started

_____

_____

_____

_____

_____

_____

_____

_____

_____

_____

_____

_____

_____

_____

_____

_____

_____

_____

_____

_____

_____

_____

_____

_____

_____

_____

_____

_____

_____

_____

# 1,000 Words to Get Started

_____ say

# 1,000 Words to Get Started

_____

_____

_____

_____

_____

_____

_____

_____

_____

_____

_____

_____

_____

_____

_____

_____

_____

_____

_____

_____

_____

_____

_____

_____

_____

_____

_____

_____

_____

# 1,000 Words to Get Started

_____ glasses

# 1,000 Words to Get Started

_____

_____

_____

_____

_____

_____

_____

_____

_____

_____

_____

_____

_____

_____

_____

_____

_____

_____

_____

_____

_____

_____

_____

_____

_____

_____

_____

_____

_____

_____

# 1,000 Words to Get Started

☐ If _____
could update

................................................................
................................................................

_____
_____
_____
_____
_____
_____
_____
_____
_____
_____
_____
_____
_____
_____
_____
_____
_____
_____
_____
_____
_____

# 1,000 Words to Get Started

# 1,000 Words to Get Started

New _____ , _____
same _____

# 1,000 Words to Get Started

# 1,000 Words to Get Started

☐ Second guess a _____

# 1,000 Words to Get Started

_____
_____
_____
_____
_____
_____
_____
_____
_____
_____
_____
_____
_____
_____
_____
_____
_____
_____
_____
_____
_____
_____
_____
_____
_____
_____
_____
_____
_____
_____
_____

# 1,000 Words to Get Started

☐ The _____
chance

# 1,000 Words to Get Started

_____
_____
_____
_____
_____
_____
_____
_____
_____
_____
_____
_____
_____
_____
_____
_____
_____
_____
_____
_____
_____
_____
_____
_____
_____
_____
_____

# 1,000 Words to Get Started

☐ Last item on _____

# 1,000 Words to Get Started

_____

_____

_____

_____

_____

_____

_____

_____

_____

_____

_____

_____

_____

_____

_____

_____

_____

_____

_____

_____

_____

_____

_____

_____

_____

_____

_____

_____

# 1,000 Words to Get Started

No one knows _____

# 1,000 Words to Get Started

# 1,000 Words to Get Started

☐ Rocky _____
  ahead

_____

_____
_____
_____

_____
_____
_____
_____
_____
_____
_____
_____
_____
_____
_____
_____
_____
_____
_____
_____
_____
_____
_____
_____

# 1,000 Words to Get Started

_____
_____
_____
_____
_____
_____
_____
_____
_____
_____
_____
_____
_____
_____
_____
_____
_____
_____
_____
_____
_____
_____
_____
_____
_____
_____
_____
_____
_____
_____

# 1,000 Words to Get Started

Different ways to say _____

# 1,000 Words to Get Started

_____

_____

_____

_____

_____

_____

_____

_____

_____

_____

_____

_____

_____

_____

_____

_____

_____

_____

_____

_____

_____

_____

_____

_____

_____

_____

_____

# 1,000 Words to Get Started

☐ Didn't _____
    that

# 1,000 Words to Get Started

_____

_____

_____

_____

_____

_____

_____

_____

_____

_____

_____

_____

_____

_____

_____

_____

_____

_____

_____

_____

_____

_____

_____

_____

_____

_____

# 1,000 Words to Get Started

☐ Last to _____

# 1,000 Words to Get Started

_____

_____

_____

_____

_____

_____

_____

_____

_____

_____

_____

_____

_____

_____

_____

_____

_____

_____

_____

_____

_____

_____

_____

_____

_____

_____

_____

_____

_____

_____

_____

_____

# 1,000 Words to Get Started

When the _____

go _____

# 1,000 Words to Get Started

_____
_____
_____
_____
_____
_____
_____
_____
_____
_____
_____
_____
_____
_____
_____
_____
_____
_____
_____
_____
_____
_____
_____
_____
_____
_____
_____
_____
_____
_____
_____
_____
_____
_____
_____
_____
_____

# 1,000 Words to Get Started

[  ] ———————————————————————— down

# 1,000 Words to Get Started

# 1,000 Words to Get Started

☐ Last _____
before closing

# 1,000 Words to Get Started

---
---
---
---
---
---
---
---
---
---
---
---
---
---
---
---
---
---
---
---
---
---
---
---
---
---
---
---
---
---
---
---
---

# 1,000 Words to Get Started

Best place for hiding _____

# 1,000 Words to Get Started

# 1,000 Words to Get Started

Final _____

# 1,000 Words to Get Started

_____
_____
_____
_____
_____
_____
_____
_____
_____
_____
_____
_____
_____
_____
_____
_____
_____
_____
_____
_____
_____
_____
_____
_____
_____
_____
_____
_____
_____
_____
_____

# 1,000 Words to Get Started

_____ outside the lines

# 1,000 Words to Get Started

_____
_____
_____
_____
_____
_____
_____
_____
_____
_____
_____
_____
_____
_____
_____
_____
_____
_____
_____
_____
_____
_____
_____
_____
_____
_____
_____
_____
_____
_____

# 1,000 Words to Get Started

☐ _____ before you
  _____

# 1,000 Words to Get Started

_____
_____
_____
_____
_____
_____
_____
_____
_____
_____
_____
_____
_____
_____
_____
_____
_____
_____
_____
_____
_____
_____
_____
_____
_____
_____
_____
_____
_____
_____

# 1,000 Words to Get Started

☐ The _____
tester

# 1,000 Words to Get Started

_____

_____

_____

_____

_____

_____

_____

_____

_____

_____

_____

_____

_____

_____

_____

_____

_____

_____

_____

_____

_____

_____

_____

_____

_____

_____

_____

_____

_____

_____

_____

# 1,000 Words to Get Started

☐ Remember _____
is cooking

# 1,000 Words to Get Started

_____

_____

_____

_____

_____

_____

_____

_____

_____

_____

_____

_____

_____

_____

_____

_____

_____

_____

_____

_____

_____

_____

_____

_____

_____

_____

_____

_____

_____

_____

# 1,000 Words to Get Started

_____ the clock

# 1,000 Words to Get Started

---
---
---
---
---
---
---
---
---
---
---
---
---
---
---
---
---
---
---
---
---
---
---
---
---
---
---

# 1,000 Words to Get Started

Along the _____

# 1,000 Words to Get Started

# 1,000 Words to Get Started

Open _____

# 1,000 Words to Get Started

_____
_____
_____
_____
_____
_____
_____
_____
_____
_____
_____
_____
_____
_____
_____
_____
_____
_____
_____
_____
_____
_____
_____
_____
_____
_____
_____
_____
_____
_____
_____

# 1,000 Words to Get Started

The first _____

# 1,000 Words to Get Started

---
---
---
---
---
---
---
---
---
---
---
---
---
---
---
---
---
---
---
---
---
---
---
---
---
---
---
---
---
---
---
---

# 1,000 Words to Get Started

[  ] _____ on top

# 1,000 Words to Get Started

_____

_____

_____

_____

_____

_____

_____

_____

_____

_____

_____

_____

_____

_____

_____

_____

_____

_____

_____

_____

_____

_____

_____

_____

_____

_____

_____

_____

_____

# 1,000 Words to Get Started

When _____
come _____

# 1,000 Words to Get Started

_____

_____

_____

_____

_____

_____

_____

_____

_____

_____

_____

_____

_____

_____

_____

_____

_____

_____

_____

_____

_____

_____

_____

_____

_____

_____

_____

_____

_____

# 1,000 Words to Get Started

Selecting _____

# 1,000 Words to Get Started

# 1,000 Words to Get Started

☐ _____ after the funeral

# 1,000 Words to Get Started

_____
_____
_____
_____
_____
_____
_____
_____
_____
_____
_____
_____
_____
_____
_____
_____
_____
_____
_____
_____
_____
_____
_____
_____
_____
_____
_____
_____
_____
_____
_____

# 1,000 Words to Get Started

□ Never _____
  again

# 1,000 Words to Get Started

_____

_____

_____

_____

_____

_____

_____

_____

_____

_____

_____

_____

_____

_____

_____

_____

_____

_____

_____

_____

_____

_____

_____

_____

_____

_____

_____

_____

_____

_____

_____

# 1,000 Words to Get Started

Creativity and _____

# 1,000 Words to Get Started

# 1,000 Words to Get Started

Across one _____

# 1,000 Words to Get Started

_____

_____

_____

_____

_____

_____

_____

_____

_____

_____

_____

_____

_____

_____

_____

_____

_____

_____

_____

_____

_____

_____

_____

_____

_____

_____

_____

_____

_____

_____

_____

_____

# 1,000 Words to Get Started

Discover the real _____

# 1,000 Words to Get Started

# 1,000 Words to Get Started

When _____

becomes _____

# 1,000 Words to Get Started

# 1,000 Words to Get Started

☐ Palpable _____
ignored

# 1,000 Words to Get Started

_____
_____
_____
_____
_____
_____
_____
_____
_____
_____
_____
_____
_____
_____
_____
_____
_____
_____
_____
_____
_____
_____
_____
_____
_____
_____
_____

# 1,000 Words to Get Started

☐ Never written _____

# 1,000 Words to Get Started

<br>
<br>
<br>
<br>
<br>
<br>
<br>
<br>
<br>
<br>
<br>
<br>
<br>
<br>
<br>
<br>
<br>
<br>
<br>
<br>
<br>
<br>

# 1,000 Words to Get Started

What happens in the _____

# 1,000 Words to Get Started

_____

_____

_____

_____

_____

_____

_____

_____

_____

_____

_____

_____

_____

_____

_____

_____

_____

_____

_____

_____

_____

_____

_____

_____

_____

_____

_____

_____

_____

# 1,000 Words to Get Started

The inventive _____

# 1,000 Words to Get Started

_____
_____
_____
_____
_____
_____
_____
_____
_____
_____
_____
_____
_____
_____
_____
_____
_____
_____
_____
_____
_____
_____
_____
_____
_____
_____
_____
_____
_____

# 1,000 Words to Get Started

Liquid _____

# 1,000 Words to Get Started

_____

_____

_____

_____

_____

_____

_____

_____

_____

_____

_____

_____

_____

_____

_____

_____

_____

_____

_____

_____

_____

_____

_____

_____

_____

_____

_____

_____

_____

# 1,000 Words to Get Started

☐ Science gone _____

# 1,000 Words to Get Started

_____
_____
_____
_____
_____
_____
_____
_____
_____
_____
_____
_____
_____
_____
_____
_____
_____
_____
_____
_____
_____
_____
_____
_____

# 1,000 Words to Get Started

☐ _____ failure

# 1,000 Words to Get Started

# 1,000 Words to Get Started

☐ A _____
design

# 1,000 Words to Get Started

# 1,000 Words to Get Started

_____ to a joke

# 1,000 Words to Get Started

_____

_____

_____

_____

_____

_____

_____

_____

_____

_____

_____

_____

_____

_____

_____

_____

_____

_____

_____

_____

_____

_____

_____

_____

_____

_____

_____

_____

_____

_____

_____

_____

_____

_____

# 1,000 Words to Get Started

When a _____
becomes a leader

# 1,000 Words to Get Started

# 1,000 Words to Get Started

☐ Coding ————————————————
  secrets

# 1,000 Words to Get Started

---
---
---
---
---
---
---
---
---
---
---
---
---
---
---
---
---
---
---
---
---
---
---
---
---
---
---
---
---
---
---
---
---
---
---
---

# 1,000 Words to Get Started

☐ Open _____,
  broken _____

# 1,000 Words to Get Started

# 1,000 Words to Get Started

_____ time in the field

# 1,000 Words to Get Started

_____

_____

_____

_____

_____

_____

_____

_____

_____

_____

_____

_____

_____

_____

_____

_____

_____

_____

_____

_____

_____

_____

_____

_____

_____

_____

_____

_____

# 1,000 Words to Get Started

☐ ——————————————— gone wrong

# 1,000 Words to Get Started

_____

_____

_____

_____

_____

_____

_____

_____

_____

_____

_____

_____

_____

_____

_____

_____

_____

_____

_____

_____

_____

_____

_____

_____

_____

_____

_____

_____

_____

_____

_____

_____

_____

# 1,000 Words to Get Started

Solutions from unlikely _____

# 1,000 Words to Get Started

_____
_____
_____
_____
_____
_____
_____
_____
_____
_____
_____
_____
_____
_____
_____
_____
_____
_____
_____
_____
_____
_____
_____
_____
_____
_____
_____
_____
_____
_____
_____
_____
_____
_____

# 1,000 Words to Get Started

Final thoughts before _____

# 1,000 Words to Get Started

_____
_____
_____
_____
_____
_____
_____
_____
_____
_____
_____
_____
_____
_____
_____
_____
_____
_____
_____
_____
_____
_____
_____
_____
_____
_____
_____
_____
_____

# 1,000 Words to Get Started

If we remembered _____

# 1,000 Words to Get Started

# 1,000 Words to Get Started

The _____
not made

# 1,000 Words to Get Started

_____
_____
_____
_____
_____
_____
_____
_____
_____
_____
_____
_____
_____
_____
_____
_____
_____
_____
_____
_____
_____
_____
_____
_____
_____
_____
_____
_____
_____
_____
_____
_____
_____

# 1,000 Words to Get Started

Fighting for _____

# 1,000 Words to Get Started

# 1,000 Words to Get Started

| | _____ ways to |

_____

# 1,000 Words to Get Started

_____
_____
_____
_____
_____
_____
_____
_____
_____
_____
_____
_____
_____
_____
_____
_____
_____
_____
_____
_____
_____
_____
_____
_____
_____
_____
_____
_____
_____

# 1,000 Words to Get Started

Writing Reflections:

_____
_____
_____
_____
_____
_____
_____
_____
_____
_____
_____
_____
_____
_____
_____
_____
_____
_____
_____
_____
_____
_____
_____
_____
_____
_____
_____
_____

# 1,000 Words to Get Started

_____

_____

_____

_____

_____

_____

_____

_____

_____

_____

_____

_____

_____

_____

_____

_____

_____

_____

_____

_____

_____

_____

_____

_____

_____

_____

# Chandra's Acknowledgments

To all the stacks of notebooks piled in my office, yearning to breathe fresh air, this one's for you.

Thank you to Zara Hoffman without whom, this entire project would not have happened. I can't thank you enough for introducing me to Natalie.

To my fabulous writing partner, Natalie Locke, who is always there to tell me the honest truth, share ideas, body double, and hear about exciting life events. Thank you for helping me to polish my word turds into shiny nuggets.

To the Flash Fiction morning crew for being up with us so many early Saturday mornings to write and share your stories. You are the best company I could ask for: Just Eva, Kat Leo, Vixen of Fiction, S. D. Huston, Carey H Author, Melissa Eick, Author J. C. Carpenter, Barrett Laurie, Spence, CherryPanda, Richard Holliday, Laura Nettles, Maggie Ward, Margaret Pinard, Cool Gamer & more.

To my fur babies, for keeping me company and reminding me that it's good to get up and stretch for a bit.

My Nickie Pooh, there aren't enough words, but thank you all the same.

And to my partner who has loved and supported me. Over the last year, there have been many things that got in the way of my writing. Thank you for being there to help shoulder the load, for listening when I was overwhelmed, and for encouraging me.

# Natalie's Acknowledgments:

I second thanks to Zara Hoffman who introduced Chandra and I to each other. I hope you don't regret the work you set for yourself with our antics.

To our entire YT family who supported our Flash Fiction Live Show: There are too many to list but a few that have stopped by or joined us on screen are Eva Blackwell, Maggie Ward, Kelli Wright, Barrett Laurie, Kate Cavenaugh, Lauren Adele, JC Carpenter, Richard Holiday, Martin Lejeune, Spence, Cherry Panda, Carey H. Author, Ken Harris, Old Grumpy Mama, Cool Gamer, CB 394, and so many more.

To Mandi Lynn: for creating our beautiful cover that we hope inspires future flash fiction writers.

And to the writers who buy this book. I hope this book helps you acknowledge your own skills and helps you pursue your goals.

# About the Authors

Chandra Arthur is a full-time rescue dog and cat mom, by day she is an IT professional, and a writer by night. She writes Science Fiction, Fantasy, and Historical fiction of full length novels, flash fiction, and everything in between. When Chandra isn't writing, you can find her pouring over a book, playing computer games, drinking coffee, and sometimes all three at once.

When Natalie isn't working, reading, taking care of two kids and two dogs with her husband, she sacrifices even more of her sleep in order to write. Letting passion be her guide, she has drafted over two hundred and fifty flash fiction pieces in fourteen months. Now she hopes to invoke passion in others.

| | | | |
|---|---|---|---|
| abacus | axle | bend | boulevard |
| above | baby | beverage | bow |
| ace | back | bicker | box |
| address | backpack | big | brace |
| adopt | backseat | bike | brag |
| afternoon | bagel | bill | break |
| agent | bail | bind | breakfast |
| ale | bake | bird | breathe |
| allergy | balance | birthmark | breed |
| alpha | bald | bite | breeze |
| angry | balk | black | brick |
| apathy | ballad | blacktop | bridge |
| apologize | band | blade | brief |
| April | banner | blank | bright |
| apron | bar | blanket | brook |
| arch | bare | blink | brunch |
| area | barrel | blob | brush |
| armchair | basic | blood | buckle |
| army | bat | bloom | buddy |
| arrive | bath | blue | bug |
| askew | beak | board | build |
| atom | beam | boat | bull |
| auction | bear | bolster | bumble |
| audience | beat | bond | bump |
| autumn | beet | bonfire | burrow |
| avenue | behold | book | bus |
| awry | believe | boot | bush |
| axe | belt | booth | bustle |

| | | | |
|---|---|---|---|
| butterfly | cavern | chop | converge |
| button | ceiling | chortle | conserve |
| buzz | celery | church | control |
| cake | cell | chute | cookie |
| calculate | cellophane | circle | corkscrew |
| calendar | cemetery | citrus | cot |
| call | chain | clean | count |
| calm | chair | clergy | cowboy |
| calorie | chaise | clock | cowlick |
| camera | chance | cloned | crack |
| camp | change | close | craft |
| candle | chant | closet | crescent |
| canyon | chapter | cloth | cringe |
| care | character | clout | crinkle |
| carnival | charisma | club | crock |
| carousel | charity | clue | crone |
| carpet | charter | cold | crop |
| carry | check | collar | cross |
| carton | cheerio | college | crumble |
| case | cherub | cologne | crunch |
| cash | child | colonel | crust |
| cashew | chime | common | cult |
| cast | chimney | complain | cupcake |
| casual | chin | complex | cure |
| cat | chip | compound | curious |
| cathedral | chocolate | concrete | curl |
| caught | choice | condition | curse |
| cave | choir | cone | curve |

| | | | |
|---|---|---|---|
| cut | disarm | egg | feline |
| cycle | distance | elevator | fence |
| czar | ditch | embargo | ferry |
| danger | dog | emblem | finger |
| dark | dome | embrace | fire |
| date | domino | emerald | first |
| day | done | emerge | flag |
| daze | door | enemy | flame |
| dazzle | double | energy | flashlight |
| deal | dough | erroneous | flee |
| declare | draft | error | flex |
| decline | dragon | escape | flight |
| deep | drain | estimate | flip |
| delicacy | drape | excite | flippant |
| deliver | dress | execute | floor |
| demon | drill | expose | flop |
| demure | drive | face | flow |
| desk | drizzle | faith | flower |
| detergent | drop | fall | fluff |
| detour | dune | family | flush |
| dew | dwell | fan | fly |
| diamond | ear | fashion | format |
| dice | earnest | faucet | found |
| different | earring | faux | fox |
| digit | earworm | fax | fracture |
| dinner | east | fear | frame |
| dinosaur | eatery | feast | free |
| dirt | eerie | feeler | freeze |

| | | | |
|---|---|---|---|
| friend | gone | hanger | hour |
| frog | gorgeous | happiness | house |
| front | grab | happy | hover |
| frown | graduate | hard | hug |
| frozen | grass | hazel | hunch |
| fun | gratitude | head | hurt |
| fur | gravel | heal | hush |
| future | gray | heel | hustle |
| gaggle | graze | height | hutch |
| gale | green | heir | hypnotic |
| game | greet | hide | ice |
| gap | grief | hike | ill |
| garage | grill | hill | incense |
| garden | grim | hit | incline |
| gate | grime | hold | inflate |
| gear | grocery | hole | inside |
| general | grow | holiday | insole |
| genius | gull | home | instance |
| ghost | gummy | hone | instant |
| gilded | gun | honey | instinct |
| give | gym | honeydew | instruct |
| glance | habit | honor | internet |
| glare | hail | hoop | item |
| glass | hair | hop | jam |
| glob | hairbrush | hope | jazz |
| glutter | half | horizontal | jean |
| gobble | hand | hospital | jerk |
| gold | handle | hotel | joint |

| | | | |
|---|---|---|---|
| juice | lay | loop | mince |
| jump | leaf | lose | miner |
| keep | league | lost | miniature |
| kelp | leap | lot | minor |
| kettle | leash | lotion | mint |
| kick | leather | luggage | minute |
| king | leave | lunch | mirror |
| kiss | leftover | major | miss |
| kit | length | make | mission |
| knife | lethal | mall | mist |
| knight | letter | map | mistake |
| knot | letterhead | march | mix |
| label | lettuce | marinate | mob |
| ladder | leverage | market | mode |
| ladylike | liberal | marry | mole |
| lake | lick | master | momentus |
| lamb | lieutenant | match | money |
| lamp | lift | may | month |
| land | light | meal | moon |
| lap | line | meat | moor |
| large | lingerie | median | morning |
| lash | lip | medicine | mosque |
| lasso | lipstick | melon | moth |
| last | list | midnight | motorcycle |
| latch | little | midyear | motto |
| lateral | live | might | mound |
| laugh | lock | milk | mountain |
| lawn | long | mimic | mouse |

| | | | |
|---|---|---|---|
| movie | opal | petal | pull |
| mow | open | pile | pulp |
| muffin | orange | pillow | punch |
| mug | order | pine | pupil |
| murder | organic | pint | push |
| museum | Orion | plain | puzzle |
| music | outside | plane | quack |
| muster | overrun | play | qual |
| muzzle | pail | plot | qualify |
| nail | pair | plow | quantify |
| naked | pal | point | queen |
| nap | pamper | polish | quest |
| near | pant | pollen | quiet |
| necklace | pantry | pond | quit |
| nest | parent | poof | quiver |
| night | park | pop | rail |
| none | parrot | possess | rain |
| north | passport | pot | rainbow |
| nose | past | prank | raisin |
| notebook | pastry | present | rake |
| number | path | price | range |
| nut | pause | pride | ransom |
| obstacle | paw | prince | rattle |
| ocean | peanut | princess | reaper |
| oil | pearl | produce | rear |
| oiler | pendulum | professor | reckless |
| Olympian | pepper | prowl | reckon |
| onstage | person | prudence | record |

| | | | |
|---|---|---|---|
| redeem | rookie | school | shock |
| reel | room | scooter | shoe |
| reflect | root | scowl | shoelace |
| relax | rot | scrape | short |
| remonstrance | rotate | scream | shot |
| repeat | rough | screen | shower |
| repertoire | round | screw | shrub |
| report | route | scroll | shrug |
| resonate | row | sea | shuffle |
| restrain | royal | search | sibling |
| resurface | ruffle | seat | side |
| retrieve | rug | second | sidewalk |
| rhyme | rule | secular | sigh |
| rib | ruminate | seldom | silo |
| riff | run | send | silver |
| right | rung | sense | sing |
| ring | rust | serial | single |
| rip | rut | shade | sink |
| ripe | sack | shake | skimp |
| ripple | safe | shape | skinned |
| rise | sage | shard | skip |
| rival | sail | share | skirt |
| river | salary | sharp | skit |
| road | sale | sheer | skyscraper |
| robe | same | sheet | slay |
| rock | sandwich | shelf | sleep |
| rogue | sapphire | shimmer | slide |
| roof | scare | ship | slip |

| | | | |
|---|---|---|---|
| slipper | splatter | straw | tablet |
| small | sport | streak | tact |
| smile | spot | stream | tadpole |
| smoke | sprain | street | take |
| smooth | sprinkle | string | tall |
| smother | sprint | stripe | tame |
| snake | squander | strobe | tank |
| snap | squeak | strong | tape |
| snare | squirm | struggle | tax |
| snoop | stadium | strut | team |
| snooty | stamp | student | tear |
| snore | staple | suite | teddy |
| snow | star | sultry | tee |
| sock | statue | summer | tell |
| soda | stay | sun | temple |
| soft | steal | support | tent |
| soil | steep | surprise | tenth |
| solicit | step | surreal | test |
| song | stitch | suspend | thick |
| sound | stock | swarm | thin |
| space | stole | swat | thistle |
| spell | stone | sway | three |
| spider | stop | swear | throne |
| spike | stoplight | sweat | tidy |
| spill | store | swim | tie |
| spin | story | switch | tie-dye |
| spine | straight | synagogue | tight |
| splat | strap | tab | tile |